An illustrated souvenir

CORNISH ENGINES

Peter Laws

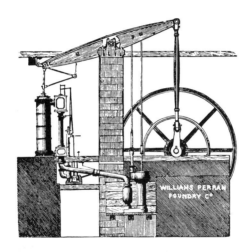

The National Trust

Introduction

If someone had predicted to the founders of the National Trust in 1895 that a steam engine (then a mere three years old and pumping water out of a Cornish tin mine) would become part of their heritage 60 years later, they would have been astonished. But this has happened, and not only one engine but five are now preserved, together with more of the tall stone buildings that housed these great machines, which were an integral part of Cornish mining for two and a half centuries.

The tin industry in Cornwall has been traced back to the Early Bronze Age (2,100–1,500BC). The first Cornish miners concentrated on washing tin ore out of deposits near the surface. By Tudor times the 'mine captains' were sinking shafts and driving complex levels through the tin-bearing strata. Steam-engines were developed by several generations of West Country engineers to pump water from these increasingly deep mines, raise ore to the surface and crush it.

At the height of the industry in the 1860s there were over 600 such engines working in Cornwall. Today only one mine, South Crofty near East Pool, is still operating commercially. The gradual decline of mining in Cornwall left a legacy of derelict buildings and engines – 'knack't bals' was the local description – which many were happy to see swept away. However, in the 1930s the Cornish Engines Preservation Society recognised the importance of saving representative examples from the period when Cornwall led the world in mining technology. The National Trust now carries on that task of preservation and explanation, with the help and encouragement of the Trevithick Society.

Restoration work under way at Levant

The pumping rod at Taylor's Shaft, East Pool

Thomas Newcomen and the early engines

Flooding has always been a threat to mining in Cornwall. In his monumental *Survey of Cornwall* (1602) Richard Carew described the difficulties facing the miners of his day:

For conveying away the Water, they pray in aide of sundry devices such as Addits [drains], Pumps and wheeles, driven by a stream; all which not withstanding the Springs so incroche upon these inventions, they are driven to keepe men and somewhere horses at work both day and night without ceasing.

In 1698–9 a Devonian mining engineer Thomas Savery produced his first 'fire engine', a steam pump for draining water from a mine shaft. The next major step forward was made by Thomas Newcomen, who has been called the father of the steam engine. His ironmonger's business in Dartmouth took him frequently into the mining areas of both Devon and Cornwall where he could see the problem of flooding for himself. By 1710 Newcomen had built an engine which was installed at the Wheal Vor (Great Work) mine near Breage, Helston. It was a failure, but two years later he designed another for a Staffordshire colliery that proved to be the world's first commercially successful steam engine. During the next 50 years Newcomen engines were put to use throughout Britain and the rest of Europe.

The Newcomen engine, like all the Cornish beam engines that succeeded it, evolved from the common backyard hand-pump still used to bring water up from the depths of a well. The hand is applied to a rod connected with a pivoted lever; as the rod is lowered, so the plunger, fixed to the other end of the lever, is raised, discharging water from the pump's spout. Newcomen substituted for the human hand a simple steam-powered piston and cylinder. Steam was admitted into the cylinder at low pressure. The cylinder was then cooled, the steam condensed, and the drop in atmospheric pressure within the chamber drove the piston into the cylinder. Samuel Smiles described Newcomen's 'atmospheric' engine in action:

... a clumsy and apparently a very painful process, accompanied by an extraordinary amount

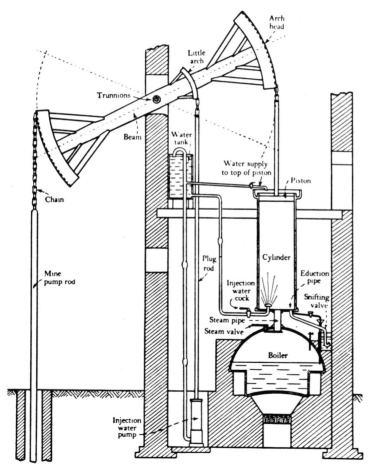

Diagram of Newcomen's 'atmospheric' engine, 1712

of wheezing, sighing, creaking, and bumping. When the pump descends, there is heard a plunge, a heavy sigh, and a loud bump: then, as it rises, and the sucker begins to act, there is heard a creak, a wheeze, another bump, and then a rush of water as it is lifted and poured out.

Because the cylinder had to be heated and cooled for each stroke, Newcomen's engine was relatively inefficient, consuming large amounts of fuel. There is no coal in Cornwall, and so, before the advent of the railways, it had to be brought by sea from South Wales at great expense; indeed it was the largest item of cost in mining. Relief came when the Scottish instrument maker James Watt invented the condenser, patented in 1765. This allowed the main cylinder to be kept hot, by drawing off steam into a separate chamber. The result was a saving of about 75% in coal. Watt also invented and patented 'parallel motion', an ingenious device for transferring power from the rocking movement of the engine beam, or 'bob', to the vertical motion of the pump rod. (It can be seen at work on the East Pool winding engine.) Watt set up in partnership with Matthew Boulton in Birmingham to manufacture the new improved engines, which were an immediate commercial success. By 1783 only one of Newcomen's 'atmospheric' engines was still working in the Cornish mines.

But this was not the end of the story. At the turn of the century the patents on Watt and Boulton's engine expired. The way was now open for a new generation of Cornish mining engineers to develop their achievements, creating the giant beam engines that were to dominate the landscape of much of Cornwall during the nineteenth century.

A late eighteenth-century 'Steam Fire Engine'

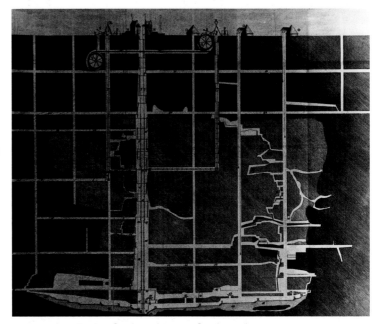

Section of the Bullen Garden mine near Camborne in 1778

Richard Trevithick and the heyday of Cornish mining

Richard Trevithick; painted by John Linnell in 1816 (Science Museum)

Richard Trevithick was born on 13 April 1771, the only son and fifth child of the manager of Wheal Chance copper mine at Roskear, near Camborne. (His birthplace is marked by a memorial stone on the side of the Pool–Carn Brea road opposite the old entrance to South Crofty mine.) Trevithick's schoolmaster reported that he was 'a disobedient, slow, obstinate, spoiled boy, frequently absent from school and very inattentive'. He spent much of his boyhood wandering about the mines and confounded those better educated than himself by solving problems intuitively rather than by the use of theory. By 1790 he was working at the Eastern Stray Park copper mine, part of the great Dolcoath complex, at a wage of one shilling a day, and his name continued to appear on the mine pay sheet for the next two years.

Trevithick brought about enormous improvements to the old Watt engines through his amazing grasp of the principles and use of high-pressure steam – what he called 'strong-steam', until then an untried source of power. Following his visits in the 1790s to the Darby Ironworks in Coalbrookdale, Shropshire, the cradle of the Industrial Revolution, he constructed his first high-pressure engine for winding ore in 1798. Darby's then built to his design the world's first locomotive, in 1802–4. He experimented with reckless abandon, using hitherto unheard of pressures of up to 100lbs per square inch, and patented his high-pressure steam engine in 1815. His Cornish confrère in this work was the blacksmith Nicholas Holman, who was born in Camborne in 1777 and founded his Boiler Works in 1801 in Pool between Camborne and Redruth.

Crucial to the success of Trevithick's engine was the boiler, of which he is reported to have said, 'My predecessors put their boiler into the fire, I have put my fire into the boiler.' This innovation led to the great Cornish engines of the early nineteenth century built by several great Cornish foundries; there is a fine example at the East Pool Whim. So successful was Trevithick's boiler development for the Cornish beam engine that the annual output of tin mined in the county rose from 2,500 tons in 1750 to 14,000 in the heyday of the industry around 1860. Engines were also required for the much larger copper mines in Cornwall. In the boom years of the 1850s about 650 beam engines were working in Cornwall, with about 60 in west Devon. These represented a colossal output from the Cornish foundries, which included, apart from Holman's, Harvey's and Sandys Vivian & Co., both near Hayle: the great Perran Foundry established in 1791 near Devoran; and the Charlestown Foundry started in 1827 by J. and R. Michell.

Between 1810 and 1815 Trevithick lived in a cottage in the village of Penponds, about a mile south-west of Camborne. It was in a very poor state indeed when the Cornish Engines Preservation Society acquired it in 1938, but since it has been taken over by the National Trust, the roof has been rethatched, new floors provided throughout and the outbuildings put in good order. The plaque on the west gable commemorating the great engineer is cast, appropriately enough, in tin.

Ever the pioneer, Trevithick left Cornwall for South America in 1816, attracted by the potential of the Peruvian silver mines. During his eleven adventurous years in Peru, Chile and Costa Rica, the torch was taken up by other Cornishmen, notably his pupil Samuel Grose (1797–1866), James Simms (1785–1862), and Michael Loam (1798–1871) and his son Matthew from Gwennap, Arthur Woolf of Camborne (1766–1837), William West (b.1805), who assisted Brunel in building the West Cornwall Railway, and Francis Michell (1780–1860), one of a dynasty of Cornish mining engineers active between 1770 and 1950.

The years 1800–70 were a period of unparalleled prosperity and change for Cornwall. Men and their families poured into the county in search of work in the tin and copper mines, the china clay works, and the foundries, quarries, railways and ports that grew with them. Between 1801 and 1861 the population rose from 192,000 to 369,000. Their efforts left an indelible mark on the landscape of Cornwall; of their way of life there is now less trace.

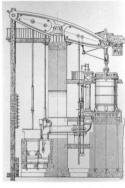

Drawing of the 80-inch Cornish Engine installed at Batter's Shaft in the West Chiverton lead mine near Zelah in the 1860s

Trevithick's cottage today

Life in the Cornish Mines

Miners at the Killifreth mine in the early 1900s

The miner's life is never easy, but working in the Cornish mines in the nineteenth century was especially hard. The temperature in the deeper mines often exceeded 100°F, the ventilation was poor, and what air there was was often filled with smoke from the blasting charges. Water streamed down the sides of the wetter shafts and the salt water in the undersea levels of the Levant mine turned the miners' skin raw red. The pitmen, kibble-fillers, trammers, sumpmen, shaftsmen, carpenters and binders each had their distinct role in the mine, working long shifts under constant threat of rock falls and flooding. Death and serious injury were commonplace. Another, more insidious danger was ankylostomiasis, or miner's anaemia, caused by a parasitic hookworm.

The hard life and the rapid cycles of boom and bust within the industry produced a nomadic breed of tough, resourceful men and women: 'a tinner has nothing to lose' was a common saying. Despite the heat, the miners chose to wear thick flannel shirts and canvas jerkins, which became stiff with tin ore and sweat. On their heads they put skullcaps and hardened felt hats, to which a candle was attached with a lump of clay; a further string of Palmer's candles hung round their necks.

By the 1840s, some of the Cornish mines were as deep as 1,500 feet, but the men were still obliged to climb up and down the shafts on ladders at the beginning and end of every shift. The more humane mine owners added platforms to the pumping rods so that miners could hitch a ride as the rod moved up and down. This crude form of lift had its dangers. In 1919 the Levant rod broke loose at the surface, killing 31

The 'man engine' at Dolcoath, photographed around 1892-3

men, the second worst accident in Cornish mining history.

On the surface the women, known as 'bal maids' or 'spallers', worked in draughty sheds or in the open air breaking up by hand the larger pieces of tin ore, before it was fed into the engine-driven stamps to break it up still further. Most of these ancillary buildings have now gone, and with them the din and vibration of the stamping hammers and the glow of the smelting furnaces, around which the bal maidens used to keep their Cornish pasties warm, despite the arsenic fumes generated by smelting that poisoned plantlife for miles around. A more peaceful reminder of that era are the remains of old railways which were designed to connect the mineheads with the ports of Portreath and Devoran.

'Bal maids' and other surface workers at the Tincroft mine in the 1890s

Decline and Rescue

Before 1870 Cornwall was the greatest tin-producing region in the world. During the next 50 years the industry was virtually wiped out. The opening up of the huge tin deposits in Malaya and Bolivia lowered the price of the metal to a level at which the Cornish mines could not compete. The local copper mines were similarly devastated by US competition and Cornish miners left home to find work abroad in vast numbers. According to one observer, 'Wherever a hole is sunk in the ground today – no matter in what corner of the globe – you will be sure to find a Cornishman at the bottom of it, searching for metal'.

Although the Cornish clung onto their mines long after others in a similar plight had closed, hundreds were eventually abandoned, their engines being sold for the price of scrap metal. By the mid-1920s there were perhaps only 20 engines left at work in Cornwall. When a very historic engine near Pendeen was about to be sold for scrap, a meeting was called at Murdoch House, Redruth, on 15 October 1935. Out of it came a Preservation Committee, whose first members included Arthur Treve Holman, Managing Director of Holman Bros., Josiah Paull, A. Pearse Jenkin, and Robert Morton Nance, Grand Bard of Cornwall. Their efforts were rewarded, for the engine was saved from the blowtorch.

In 1943 the Cornish Engines Preservation Society, which had evolved from the 1935 meeting, published a report that advocated preserving, as part of Britain's historic heritage of mechanical power, twelve Cornish beam engines, of which seven or eight were then still working. The Society managed to save several examples,

but concern about the rapid disappearance of the other surviving engines mounted, when in 1955 the Chief Inspector of Ancient Monuments of the Ministry of Works admitted that it was unlikely to be able to help, important though these engines undoubtedly were. With the future of the Society in some doubt, in 1964 the National Trust offered to accept the task of preservation, if funds to repair the buildings and endow them for the future could be found. The money was raised from an HBC grant of £3,000 and by a national appeal, to which the Cornwall County Council and the Camborne-Redruth Urban District Council both gave substantial support. In 1967 the National Trust took over the Society's Cornish engines. Since 1984 the Society, reborn as the Trevithick Society, has been working with the Trust to restore the Levant engine.

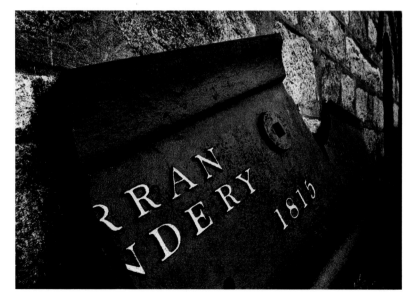

Fragment of a shattered engine bob at Taylor's Shaft, East Pool

The late Ronnie Alford and Milton Thomas at work on the beam of the Levant engine

The Engines – East Pool Whim

The most prominent beam engine to be seen in Cornwall today is the East Pool Whim on the south side of the A3047 at Pool – a fitting introduction to the Cornish Engines in the Trust's possession. 'Whim' comes from 'whimsey', an early nineteenth-century term for a winding engine. The old East Pool Mine was a venture of this period that yielded great dividends, and this engine was designed by Francis Michell for winding at the mine, drawing both miners and ore from a depth of 1,500 feet. It was the last one to be built by Holman Bros., at their Camborne foundry in 1887. The cylinder is 30 inches in diameter and the stroke is unusually long at nine feet. There was a sister engine nearby and both were very economical in fuel, using only seven hundredweight of coal a day. The shaft, known as Michell's, was 40 yards to the east of the engine house.

A story told by the late John Trounson of Redruth about this engine illustrates the dangers of the industry:

On one occasion the driver was hoisting men up the shaft, the engine going at full speed, when he suddenly realised with horror that the cage was likely to go right up through the top of the head frame. He just could not have been watching his indicator that clearly showed where the cage was in relation to the shaft. There was simply no time to shut off steam and apply the brake for the cage was too near the top and even a few seconds delay would have meant it going over the wheel and the men thrown out. With considerable presence of mind, the driver slammed in the reversing lever with the result that the engine stopped almost instantaneously, shearing the great crankshaft in two and doing a vast amount of damage. The cage was in fact within a few feet of the winding wheel when it stopped; to be followed by a very short prayer meeting up there and then a rush of miners into the engine house where the blasphemy broke all records!

On 18 May 1921 an enormous underground movement of rock destroyed Michell's shaft

East Pool Whim around 1895

and so the engine's life came to an end. The mine itself closed the following year. The engine was saved from the wartime scrap metal drive in 1941 by Arthur Treve Holman, but by 1946 it was in a sorry state. The top of the chimneystack had fallen through the roof; the windows had been smashed by vandals and all the bright parts were blackened and dirty.

After the Trust took over in 1967, it thoroughly repaired the engine and its house, and later decided to add a boiler house to house a Hornsby steam boiler taken out of the old Truro workhouse. On 20 August 1975 the splendidly restored engine was set in motion once again, although driven by electricity rather than steam.

The steam boiler at East Pool Whim

East Pool Whim today

The Pumping Engine at Taylor's Shaft, East Pool Mine

Taylor's Shaft engine house

Just across the main road from the East Pool Whim is Trevithick Road, and away to the east at its northern end lies the building that houses the largest and youngest of all the engines left in Cornwall, the Pumping Engine at Taylor's Shaft.

This great engine, its cylinder 90 inches in diameter, weighs 125 tons. It was commissioned in 1891 at a cost, including boilers and capstan, of £5,500. The designer was Nicholas Trestrail, the builders Harvey & Co. of Hayle, and it was set to work in 1892 at the Highburrow East Shaft at the nearby Carn Brea Mine, then a profitable venture that had produced in 55 years about £2.5m worth of copper, tin ore and some arsenic.

The engine was silenced in 1913 when the mine failed. A decade later it was bought by East Pool and Agar Ltd for pumping from a new shaft then being sunk and known as Taylor's, after the manager. (The initials of the company appear on the chimneystack.) A brand new engine house, surely the last one ever to be built in Cornwall, was erected in 1924. The date is on the keystone of the arch on the 'bob wall' and the engine was installed in that year. It began pumping in 1925 and continued day in and day out for nearly 30 years.

The East Pool machine, the largest standard size, represents the peak of development of the Cornish Beam pumping engine at the end of the nineteenth century. Its piston stroke in the cylinder is ten feet but, as the bob is pivoted off-centre, the stroke in the pumping rod is nine feet. The huge double bob, 33 feet long, alone weighs 52 tons, and its fulcrum rests on padstones set in a granite wall 80 inches thick.

Attached to the outer end of the beam is the timber and iron pumping rod that once descended into the shaft for a distance of 1,700 feet. Attached to it were pump rams and valves at intervals of about 240 feet. In order to assist the engine in raising this immense dead weight, counterbalances, or balance-boxes, were connected to the rod 300 feet, 900 feet and 1,425 feet down the shaft. They operated rather like seesaws, with one end attached to the pumping rod, the other fixed to a large metal container full of lumps of rock and metal. As the rod began its travel upwards, lifted by the great engine, the heavy box on the seesaw moved downwards. The balance box that can be

The East Pool Pumping Engine 'in work' in July 1951

Taylor's Shaft engine house and chimneystack

seen at ground level was installed as late as 1946. The total weight of water in motion in the shaft at every engine stroke was 84.7 tons, and with a stroke every 12 seconds, about 27,000 gallons were pumped out of the mine every hour (92 gallons per stroke).

The East Pool and Agar Mine finally closed in October 1945, and the engine was then worked by the adjacent South Crofty Mine in order to prevent its levels being flooded. One morning in October 1953 fractures were noticed in the headgear; at 6 o'clock that evening the 80-foot structure crashed to the ground. The great beam engine was doing its job of raising and lowering the 1,700-foot-long pumping rod, when loud cracking noises were heard and, with practically no warning, the gear started to crumble. The engineer on duty had the presence of mind to stop the engine.

Connecting the balance-bob with the pump rod is an engine bob from the last complete beam engine ever to be made in Cornwall. It was a 36-inch engine made by the Charlestown Foundry, St Austell, in 1911, for pumping clay slurry at the North Goonbarrow clay works near Bugle. When it was taken out of service, South Crofty purchased the beam and it did duty at Taylor's Shaft for the last eight years of the life of the engine.

This magnificent pump, serviced by five Cornish boilers operating at a steam pressure of 50lbs per square inch, came to the end of its working life at 11.30am on 28 September 1955, and there were tear-filled eyes amongst its engine room staff that morning. It was saved from the scrap heap through the generosity of Greville Bath, an American engineering historian of international repute.

The cylinder head of Taylor's Engine

Taylor's Engine valve gear

Taylor's Engine beam

Robinson's Engine, South Crofty Mine

Three-quarters of a mile south-west of the two East Pool engines was the last active mine in Cornwall, South Crofty, which until 2001 produced tin, copper and zinc after generations of mining in this part of the Camborne-Redruth district. Until December 1950 there were two beam engines at this mine, a 90-inch designed by Matthew Loam and built at Harvey's Foundry, Hayle, in the 1870s, reputedly for a Welsh colliery, and the much older 80-inch, pumping water from Robinson's Shaft. The 90-inch broke up in steam in December 1950, when the 48-ton bob snapped because of overloading, but the

Robinson's Shaft engine survived to complete over a century of working life.

Robinson's engine was commissioned from the Copperhouse Foundry near Hayle in 1853, then owned by Sandys, Vivian & Co. Throughout its 45-year life the foundry turned out pumping engines, steam locomotives and suspension bridges. Robinson's engine was designed by the engineer Captain Samuel Grose, who was born to Cornish parents in 1791 at Nether Stowey in west Somerset and was apprenticed to Trevithick. He died in 1866, and this engine was one of the last he designed.

The engine has had a complicated

Detail of the equilibrium valve on Robinson's Engine

The engine beam is covered in grease to prevent it rusting

history. It first worked Davy's Shaft at Great Wheal Alfred (or Alfred Consols) Mine near Hayle in June 1854. When that mine closed in 1864, it was moved to Crenver and Wheal Abraham Mine five miles away to the south-east, and re-erected at Pelly's Shaft. Here it worked for eleven years until 1875, when the pump rod broke and the piston shattered the cylinder. In 1882 the usable parts were again taken down. Forty-five horses pulled the 37-ton iron beam, together with the rest of the engine, across country to Tregurtha Downs, a mine just east of Marazion well-known for the quality of its tin. In an immense new engine house, still to be seen to the north of the B3280 west of Goldsithney, it was re-erected at St Aubyn's Shaft and was required to pump at the incredibly fast rate of 13 strokes a minute, as the Tregurtha Downs group of mines was always very wet.

It survived a spectacular fire during the night of 4 January 1889, started by a boy who dropped a candle into some waste lying in the middle chamber. The smouldering fire was not discovered until 4am and it took the Marazion fire brigade, consisting of a sergeant and one man, 45 minutes to gallop across to the mine with their horse-drawn engine. Unfortunately, their primitive equipment broke down before they had even started to tackle the blaze. A boy was then sent on horseback to Penzance for its brigade, which reached the fire at 9am. The Penzance firemen could do nothing but watch the embers of the engine house crumble away. Three hundred hands were out of work, but so great was the determination of the Company, that the house was rebuilt and the engine in work again within a fortnight.

After the mine closed about 1897–8, the engine lay derelict for several years. It was eventually purchased by South Crofty Ltd in September 1902 for £375, a tenth of its original price. Messrs J. & W. Gay built a new engine house for it in 1903, using stone taken partly from three old engine houses. Later that year the engine, now in its 50th year, was again put to work, and it continued to pump 340 gallons a minute from a depth of 2,021 feet night and day until it was over 100 years old. It finally stopped work at 1.03 pm on 1 May 1955. South Crofty Ltd gave it to the Preservation Society, which repaired it as a memorial to the late Arthur Treve Holman. It has been mothballed to prevent deterioration, and access is restricted. It is hoped to open it more fully when circumstances permit.

The Robinson's Engine equilibrium valve

Rostowrack Engine

Designed by William West, this engine was made by West & Sons at their St Blazey foundry in 1851, soon after the works were established, and was installed for pumping at a clay works at Locking Gate, near Bugle, to the north of St Austell. Here it stayed until 1860. In the following year it was moved to the Rostowrack clay works nearby, where it did duty continuously for 91 years until 1952, an amazing feat for steam power.

This is known technically as a single-action 22-inch cylinder rotative engine. Most such rotative engines, with their big sweep arm or connecting rod (sometimes called the pitman) between the outer end of the beam and the fly-wheel shaft, were used for winding purposes. The Rostowrack engine, however, was a pumping engine, the circular motion of the sweep arm being translated into the up-and-down action of the pump rod by the use of a bellcrank and flat rods. Its flywheel shaft made of hand-laminated iron came originally from an engine at St Erth, probably made at the Treloweth Mills, and fitted c.1890.

When the time came for this engine to be retired, the Goonvean & Rostowrack China Clay Co. Ltd, whose Chairman was Lord Falmouth (at the time President of the Cornish Engines Preservation Society), gave it to the Society and, through the kindness of Holman Bros., it was re-erected in their museum in 1953. After Holman Bros. was taken over by another company, this splendid museum was, sadly, closed, and the engine, which had worked by compressed air, was dismantled. It is now at Wheal Edward mine, Troon, near Camborne.

Rinsey

On the coast of Mount's Bay, between Porthleven and Praa Sands are three engine houses, two at Trewavas Head, part of Wheal Trewavas, an undersea copper mine (pre-1838–c.1850) and the fine engine house built in 1860 at Wheal Prosper above Rinsey Cove. This mine was part of the Marazion Mines group, and yielded 14,600 tons of copper ore between 1832 and 1849. According to J.H. Collins, the authority on West of England mining, it was not a tin mine, but small quantities of tin and lead ores were extracted from other mines in the group. Wheal Prosper was occasionally part of Prosper United and Wheal Rinsey. It finally ceased operations in 1865.

The shaft immediately adjoining the building on the seaward side was 100 fathoms deep (600 feet), and when the Trust acquired it in 1969, it was faced with a problem of a building that had been

The Rostowrack Engine 'in work' about 1948

showing serious signs of collapse as far back as 1960. Mindful of its heritage (and such buildings are as much a part of Cornish history as are windmills to that of East Anglia), the Trust decided to restore the house and launched a public appeal. Messrs. R.T. Pascoe & Son of Breage contracted to restore it, and cap the shaft; work started in November 1970, and was completed the following year.

The engine house was built of local yellow killas (clay slate) with granite dressings, and to replace important quoins, several were recovered from the ruins at Levant Mine. An old local quarry near by was even re-opened to obtain the right stone, and care was taken to use only Gwithian sand in order to produce mortar of the correct texture and colour.

The Rinsey engine house

Cape Cornwall Mines

There are only two capes on the island comprising England, Wales, Cornwall and Scotland: Cape Wrath in Sutherland and Cape Cornwall. The latter is a gem, a beautiful landscape that is also rich in archaeological sites and the remains of tin and copper mining from the past 200 years.

For many years the National Trust had sought unsuccessfully to acquire this important landmark, and so it was the cause for rejoicing in 1987 when 78 acres, including one and a half miles of coastline, were purchased by H.J. Heinz Ltd through its 'Guardians of the Countryside' scheme and then given to the Trust to preserve for ever. It is a unique place and to very many the 'connoisseur's Land's End', offering a distinctive sense of peace, without the commercialism of Land's End itself.

There were once four main mines at Cape Cornwall – from north to south, Wheal Castle, Bosweddan, Cape Cornwall and St Just Amalgamated. The last was large enough to have two pumping engines, one also driving 36 stampheads, and two winding engines. This group of mines included a mass of smaller ones bearing curious names such as Little Bounder, Bellon, Venton, Prase, Yankee Boy, Wheal Call and Wheal Cunning. Wheal Cunning started in 1872 and had three pumping, two stamping and two winding engines, and in addition a very great amount of water-powered machinery. The greatest machine of all was a water-wheel 65 feet in diameter, second only to the 72-foot giant, the *Lady Isabella* at Laxey lead mine on the Isle of Man, which is still extant. The Wheal Cunning wheel pit, massively constructed, also remains as a mute reminder of nineteenth-century Cornish water engineering.

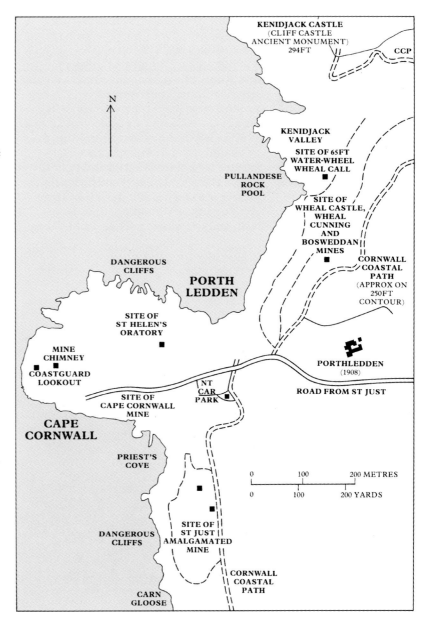

Cape Cornwall and its mine, with St Just United or Amalgamated Mine in the foreground, *c.*1900

Levant Engine

The Levant engine in 1968

The name Levant is known to Cornish miners all over the world. The grim granite cliffs that face the Atlantic north of St Just have been mined for tin and copper for perhaps twenty centuries, but the great mining venture at Levant only started in 1820 and lasted 110 years; a further chapter in its history was written by its underground link-up with Geevor mine near by in 1966–8.

The surviving Levant engine was designed by Francis Michell and built in 1840 at Harvey's Foundry in Hayle. The cylinder is 27 inches and the stroke four feet. The engine wound ore from Skip Shaft, and the winding drums can be seen on the seaward side of the engine house. The engine wound two skips up and down the shaft at a speed of 400 feet per minute. The skip was a rectangular iron box with wheels running on guide rails down the shaft, which was 290 fathoms deep (1,140 feet), but the main tramming level for filling the skip with ore was at the 278 fathom level (1,068 feet). The workings of this mine extended for a mile out underneath the Atlantic. Skip Shaft was both narrow and crooked, as the author can testify, having descended its depths in 1973.

Mining at Levant stopped in 1930 and a firm of demolition contractors moved onto

Levant Mine about 1902. The 1840 engine house is on the left and next to it is the mine pumping engine, made by Harvey's in 1835 and scrapped a century later

24

the site, having purchased the plant for scrap. W. A. Michell, the designer's grandson, and W. Tregoning Hooper, who visited the mine in August 1935, noted with regret that the work of dismantling the very old winding engine had begun. They felt that an effort must be made to preserve, if nothing else, this particular engine as a memorial to a period when Cornish engineers were in the forefront of engine design. Mr Hooper then raised £25 towards the purchase and the campaign got under way.

After their initial meeting in Redruth in October 1935, the Preservation Committee appealed for £300 to buy the engine to save it from the scrapheap. The money came in, the engine was saved and thus began the conservation of Cornish industrial monuments that has since taken a far more significant turn. Because of that meeting one old engine was saved, but out of it there has come the much wider movement to safeguard many more artefacts of the Cornish Industrial Revolution. Today interest in industrial archaeology is nationwide.

This isolated engine house, on the extreme edge of the cliff one mile west of Pendeen, was subjected to vandalism and became costly to maintain. In 1985 a team of volunteers drawn from the Trevithick Society – christened 'the Greasy Gang' – began to refurbish this historic engine, while the National Trust restored the building itself. In 1989 an appeal was launched to help put the engine back in steam, although, for practical reasons, the engine is currently powered by a concealed modern plant fired by oil. The engine re-opened in 1992 and now can be visited with the nearby Geevor mine, which is managed by Pendeen Community Heritage.

The Greasy Gang take a break from work on restoring the Levant engine

Carn Galver Mine

Between 1957 and 1987 almost 750 acres of magnificent landscape worthy of a National Park were acquired by the Trust in West Penwith, comprising one and a half miles of granite cliffs between Porthmeor Cove and Trevean in the western part of Zennor parish, and the hinterland up to Little Galver and Hannibal's Carn above 760 feet. These hills are known as 'Bosigran and Rosemergy' from the farms of those names.

To the north-east, a further 32 acres came to the Trust in 1982, comprising the Celtic hill-castle of Trereen Dinas and Gurnard's Head. Both places contain relics of nineteenth-century mining.

On the headland itself, Gurnard's Head copper mine was operating in the 1830s, relying entirely for its power on a 20-inch-wide water-wheel. It gave employment to 25 but has long since ceased working. The Porthmeor valley to the west contains a wealth of mining remains, including water-wheel pits and circular 'buddles' (ore-washing sites).

Near the hamlet of Rosemergy are two old buildings of Carn Galver (or Galva) tin mine alongside the B3306 coast road (St Ives–St Just). The mine was part of the group known as Morvah and Zennor United that included Morvah Hill mine.

The two engine houses at Carn Galver contained a pumping engine that drew water from the 130-fathom (780-foot) shaft of this very wet mine, and a second engine used to raise and crush ore. The latter was fitted with two pneumatic stamps that did the work of sixteen of the ordinary kind. Carn Galver mine ceased working about 1878. All these buildings are described in more detail in leaflet 10, 'West Penwith', in the *Coast of Cornwall* series.

The Carn Galver engine houses today

The beam winding and pumping engines at Carn Galver about 1880

St Agnes

On the edge of the cliff, west of St Agnes Beacon and due north of Chapel Porth, lies the deserted Wheal Coates mine that produced mainly tin, but also a little copper. Along the coastal footpath and almost 200 feet above the sea is the pumping engine house of the Towanwroath shaft, which is 106 fathoms (636 feet) deep. From the beach at low water, the lode is visible on the cliff face. In the schedule of working mines published in June 1873, it is stated that the company working this mine had started the previous year and had erected new pumping, winding and stamping engines. The Towanwroath engine house and the ruins of the winding and stamps engine houses higher up the cliff are therefore likely to have been built in 1872–3. The winding engine house is red and black in colour, the latter possibly a kind of gabbro, or igneous rock, quarried from underground, and so different from the stone used at Wheal Prosper. The mine stopped working in 1889, but there was an attempt to re-open it in 1911; final closure came on 17 March 1914. Inside the stone stamps engine house is a massive concrete engine bed, of this last period. The pumping engine house is a distinctively Cornish addition to the magnificent coast scenery.

In Chapel Porth itself, where the Trust has provided a free car-park, a path leads up the valley half a mile to the ruined engine house of a mine called North Towan, later part of Wheal Charlotte. This may have been built in the 1830s, when copper ore was being mined. Visitors should beware of a very deep pit at the side of the building, which is probably the site of the mine-shaft.

The Wheal Coates engine house

The Wheal Coates winding and stamps engine houses

28

Pentireglaze

One mile south of Towanwroath and on the cliff top, is another engine house of Wheal Charlotte. On the Trust's land here, which totals 363 acres, there is also a huge tract of old mining waste, interspersed with many old shafts, that extends from Towan Cross on the Porthtowan–St Agnes road to the coast at Mulgram Hill, and covers about two miles of coastline south of St Agnes Head. This tract of land is fully described in 'St Agnes and Chapel Porth', *Coast of Cornwall* leaflet 8.

On this headland overlooking Pentireglaze Haven, three and a half miles NNE of Padstow on the east side of the Camel Estuary, are the 'burrows' or 'deads' of the ancient Pentireglaze mine that produced antimony and lead. Antimony was used to harden the lead from which printer's type-metal has traditionally been made. The mine was also famous for its specimen of cerusite (lead carbonate). It has been traced back over 400 years ago and was last worked about 1857.

The Towanwroath engine house

Engines outside Cornwall

The west of England mining region extended east out of Cornwall as far as the Brendon Hills iron mines in north-west Somerset. Throughout most of the nineteenth century the Tamar Valley was extraordinarily rich in copper and other minerals, and Tavistock was the west Devon centre of the Stannaries, the ancient court and parliament of the West Country tinners.

Wheal Betsy

Four miles north-east of Tavistock on the A386 (the main road to Okehampton), and lying below and to the east of the road, is the splendid beam engine house of Wheal Betsy. A tremendous back-cloth is formed by Dartmoor to the east, and Gibbet Hill rising to 1,158 feet on the west.

North-east of the building, a stream rises at Chalwell, which provided sufficient head of water to turn two 50-foot water-wheels after the mine was re-opened in 1806. The ore raised was lead with traces of silver. In 1868 the engine house was built to house a large beam engine, which continued in use until the mine closed in 1877. In earlier years, the miners raised 400 tons of ore a year, yielding 4–5,000 ounces of silver.

After electricity nationalisation, the engine house came into the possession of the South-Western Electricity Board, which was asked by the Army for permission to blow it up as a military exercise. There was, rightly, a public outcry, and the building was given to the Cornish Engines Preservation Society, which in turn offered it to the Trust in 1967. A grant from the Historic Buildings Council enabled the Trust to restore the engine house in 1968. To the south-west of the engine house, along the sides of the valley, can be seen extensive remains of mine workings.

Left and above: the Wheal Betsy engine house